EAST COAST
RIVERS

FROM THE AIR

SECOND COLLECTION

EAST COAST RIVERS FROM THE AIR
SECOND COLLECTION
ISBN 0-948788-41-0

Cover photographs:
front - Entrance to the River Deben at Felixstowe Ferry
back - The Chapel of St. Peters-on-the-Wall at Bradwell-Juxta-
         Mare.

Published by Barnacle Marine Limited

Originated printed and bound by
Regent Publishing Services Hong Kong Ltd.

Contents

Introduction to the Second Collection

Encouraged by the reception given to the first collection of aerial photographs of the rivers and creeks of the Thames Estuary, I decided that rather than simply reprint the book, I would take a new series of photographs of a different set of locations.

The River Medway and the Swale were not well represented in the first book, so that imbalance has been corrected by including shots of Gillingham, Cockham Woods, Queenborough, Conyer and Oare Creek.

Marinas have become such an important part of sailing today that I have included photographs showing the new yacht harbours at Burnham-on-Crouch and Shotley Point in Harwich Harbour. Judging by the comments of those who bought the first edition, many of them enjoyed spotting their own boats in a marina or on a mooring and I think some of the views included this time will enable more yachtsmen to single out their craft.

For those interested in the histories of Essex or Suffolk, several photographs warrant special mention. The shot from above Orford shows both the castle built for Charles II between 1165 and 1173 and St. Bartholomew's church of the same period. The tower of the church is some twenty feet higher than the keep of the castle, but on a clear day the views from either are splendid and are well worth the climb.

I was particularly pleased with the photograph taken from above the Dengie Flats because it includes the ancient Chapel of St. Peter's on the Wall and seems to me to have captured something of the solitude of this remote edge of Essex, where the Romans built their fort of Othona towards the end of the third century.

The photograph of Mistley clearly shows Robert Adam's twin church towers and reminds us of Richard Rigby's ambitious scheme to turn the place into a fashionable eighteenth century resort.

All the photographs used in the first book were taken around the time of high water and some yachtsmen expressed disappointment because there was no evidence of the shoals that often trap the unwary in the shallow waters of the Thames Estuary. So, this time I decided to cover the entrances to the Ore and the Deben fairly near low water so that some idea of the configuration of the off-lying shingle knolls could be gained. However I must stress once again that all such shoals are everchanging and this book of photographs is certainly not intended to replace *East Coast Rivers* as a yachtsman's pilot.

Unlike Patrick Roach and Andrew Bray, who obtained all of the shots I used in the first book during a single flight, I and my two helpful pilots; Graham Jones from Ipswich and Edward Clack from Southend, had to make several sorties to obtain the views I needed. The vagaries of the weather concern the aerial photographer just as much as the yachtsman.

If you would like to have an enlarged colour print made from any of the original transparencies used for the illustrations in the book, contact Barnacle Marine, Blomfield Place, 25 St. Botolph's Street, Colchester, Essex CO2 7EA.
Tel: (0206) 760555

INDEX MAP
TO
PHOTOGRAPHS

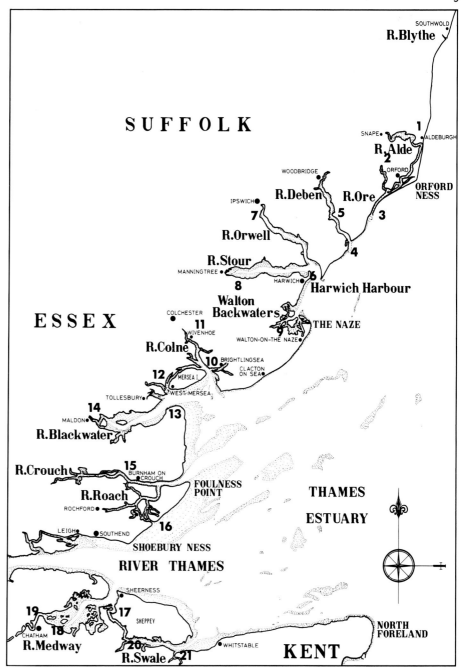

NORTH SEA

ALDEBURGH

ALDEBURGH Y.

ALBEBURGH MARSHES

THE QUAY

WESTROW REACH

1. RIVER ALDE (*Slaughden Quay*)
Descriptive notes on page 50

NORTH SEA

LIGHTHOUSE

LANTERN MARSHES

ORFORD S.C.   THE QUAY

ST. BARTHOLOMEW'S

THE CASTLE

2.   RIVER ORE (Orford)
Descriptive notes on page 50

ORFORD NESS

HOLLESLEY BAY

NORTH WEIR POINT

BEACON

COASTGUARD COTTAGE

SHINGLE STREET

OXLEY MARSHES

3. **RIVER ORE** *(Shingle Street)*
Descriptive notes on page 51

MARTELLO TOWER

BAWDSEY SHORE

'FERRYBOAT INN'

FELIXSTOWE FERRY S.C.

GOLF COURSE

BOATYARD

4. RIVER DEBEN *(Felixstowe Ferry)*
Descriptive notes on page 51

HOO ST. WERBURGH

SAXON SHORE WAY

HOO MARINA

SHORT REACH

HOO NESS

GILLINGHAM REACH

GILLINGHAM MARINA

ENTRANCE LOCK

17. **RIVER MEDWAY** (Gillingham Marina)

KINGSNORTH JETTY

HOO MARINA

COCKHAM WOODS

MEDWAY Y.C.

ST. MARY'S ISLAND

UPNOR S.C.

WHARF

18. RIVER MEDWAY (Cockham Reach)

GRAIN TOWER

SHEERNESS

THE LAPPEL

QUEENBOROUGH POINT

QUEENBOROUG

RUSHENDEN MARSHES

19. THE SWALE *(Queenborough)*

THE QUAY

BOATYARD

THE DOCK

'SHIP INN'

BOATYARD

20. THE SWALE (Conyer Quay)

HARTY FERRY

EAST SWALE

NAGDEN MARSHES

FAVERSHAM CREEK

'SHIPWRIGHT'S ARM

HOLLOW SHORE

OARE CREEK

21. THE SWALE *(Oare Creek)*

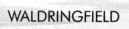

WALDRINGFIELD

THE TIPS

THE ROCKS

RAMSHOLT CHURCH

'RAMSHOLT ARMS'

THE QUAY

5. RIVER DEBEN *(Ramsholt)*

Descriptive notes on page 52

GUARD BUOY

LANDGUARD POINT

THE SHELF

DOVERCOURT BREAKWATER

HARWICH

THE POUND

ENTRANCE LOCK

SHOTLEY POINT MARINA

6. HARWICH HARBOUR (*Shotley Point Marina*)
Descriptive notes on page 52

LOCK GATES

CONTAINER TERMINAL

IPSWICH

POWER STATION

CLIFF REACH

ORWELL Y.C.

FOX'S MARINA

BOURNE BRIDGE

7. RIVER ORWELL (Ipswich)
Descriptive notes on page 53

SEAFIELD BAY

SHIP BREAKERS YARD

BALTIC WHARF

MALTHOUSES

STATION

THE QUAY

ADAM'S TOWERS

8. RIVER STOUR (Mistley)
Descriptive notes on page 53

HAMFORD WATER

STONE POINT

WALTON CHANNEL

HEDGE END ISLAND

THE TWIZZLE

TICHMARSH MARINA

9. **WALTON BACKWATERS** *(Tichmarsh Marina)*
Descriptive notes on page 54

CLACTON

ST. OSYTH CREEK

CINDERY ISLAND

WHARF

HARD

FERRY LANDING

ST. OSYTH POINT

WESTMARSH POINT

10. RIVER COLNE (Brightlingsea)

Descriptive notes on page 54

COLCHESTER

ROWHEDGE

'THE ANCHOR'

STATION

ROMAN RIVER

'ROSE & CROWN'

OLD FERRY HARD

SHIPYARD

11. **RIVER COLNE** (Wivenhoe)
Descriptive notes on page 55

PYEFLEET

THE STROOD

THE RAY

WEST MERSEA Y.C.

'THE VICTORY'

BOATYARD

PONTOON

BESOM FLEET

PACKING MARSH ISLAND

COBMARSH ISLAND

THE QUARTER

SALTCOTT CREEK

12. RIVER BLACKWATER (West Mersea)
Descriptive notes on page 55

RIVER BLACKWATER

ATOMIC POWER STATION

PEWIT ISLAND

QUAY

BRADWELL QUAY Y.C.

GREEN MAN

SAILING CENTRE

BRADWELL CREEK

BRADWELL MARINA

13. RIVER BLACKWATER (Bradwell Marina)
Descriptive notes on page 56

THE CANAL

HEYBRIDGE

'OLD SHIP'

'JOLLY SAILOR'

BOATYARD

THE BASIN

THE LOCK

LOCK-KEEPER

14. RIVER BLACKWATER *(Heybridge Basin)*

BURNHAM MARINA

CROUCH Y.C.

BOATYARD

'WHITEHART'

TOWN QUAY

ROYAL BURNHAM Y.C.

ROYAL CORINTHIAN Y.C.

15. BURNHAM-ON-CROUCH
Descriptive notes on page 57

RIVER ROACH

BARLING CREEK   FORD

POTTON ISLAND

POTTON BRIDGE

THE MIDDLEWAY

RUSHLEY ISLAND

THE NARROWS

HAVENGORE CREEK

HAVENGORE BRIDGE

16. RIVER ROACH (*Havengore Bridge*)

DESCRIPTIVE
NOTES
and
PRACTICAL
INFORMATION

1. SLAUGHDEN QUAY *(Aldeburgh)*

Any aerial photograph of Slaughden Quay, where the River Alde turns abruptly inland, serves as a graphic reminder of the extreme proximity of the North Sea. The sea wall hereabouts is now being reinforced, to the understandable relief of many people living in the area, as well as members of the two sailing clubs that have their headquarters at the Quay.

The river, which rises several miles inland near a place called Brundish, remains the Alde until it reaches Orford, some four or five miles to the south; after which it becomes the Ore and as such enters the sea at Orford Haven, off Shingle Street.

Crabbe, the poet who was born in Aldeburgh in 1754, wrote some lines that describe many East Coast rivers as well as his native Alde:
'With ceaseless motion comes and goes the tide
Flowing, it fills the channel vast and wide;
Then back to sea, with strong majestic sweep
It rolls, in ebb yet terrible and deep;

Here Samphire-banks and Salt-wort bound the flood
There stakes and sea-weeds withering on the mud;
And higher up, a ridge of all things base,
Which some strong tide has roll'd upon the place.'

Since 1948, Aldeburgh has been famed for its Annual Festival of Music and Arts, based nowadays at the Maltings Concert Hall at Snape Bridge which can be reached by water only on a flood tide and with a great deal of sounding. Aldeburgh Yacht Club, formed in 1897, is sited so that competitors in their races can be watched for quite a distance either along Westrow or Home Reach. The classes they race range from Squibs to Dragons, some of which are built at Peter Wilson's yard just up the road.

Tides
HW at Slaughden Quay is 1hr. 55min. after HW Dover.
Range of tide at Springs: 2.3m; at Neaps: 2m.

Charts
Admiralty No.2052.
Stanfords No.6 (The Suffolk Rivers).

Facilities
For moorings contact Upson's yard at Quay.
Fuel from yard or garages in town.
Water: at Quay
Chandlery from Aldeburgh Yacht Co.
Clubs: Aldeburgh YC and Slaughden Quay SC.

Points of interest
At Aldeburgh: Moot Hall and RNLI Lifeboat Station.
At Snape: Maltings Festival Hall.

Sustenance
Hotels and restaurants in Aldeburgh.
The Maltings and 'Plough and Sail' at Snape Bridge.

2. ORFORD *(Looking East)*

Until the middle of the 12th century there were no Royal castles in Norfolk or Suffolk, only those owned by barons. So, in 1165, Henry II decided to build Orford Castle, the keep of which can be clearly seen in this photograph. The castle was built largely of septaria stone, known as 'Roman cement', and timber shipped south from Scarborough. Septaria was dredged from the bottom off the Suffolk and Essex coasts and at one time as many as fifty smacks were at work gathering the stone.

Equally prominent is the tower of St. Bartholomew's, built about the same time as the castle, but on the site of an earlier Norman Church.

Not quite so easily spotted in the photograph is the red and white tower of the lighthouse on Orfordness, marking the easternmost point on the English coast. There has been a light on this spot since the early 17th century, although the present 90 foot structure dates from 1793. Many a yachtsman, returning from the Low Countries or Scandinavia has been comforted by the sight

of the Orford light flashing at five second intervals while he was still twenty miles or more out in the North Sea.

The yachts now moored off Orford Quay are some four or five miles from the entrance to the river at Shingle Strret; but maps show that in the time of Henry VIII, the entrance was opposite the castle – probaly towards the right hand edge of this photograph – while wharves extended all along Quay Street almost up to the Church. The many warehouses have long since gone, but the 'Jolly Sailor' remains as popular today with yachtsman as it has been with other seaman over the centuries.

The land on the eastern side of the river opposite Orford, known as the Lantern Marshes, is a 'no-go' area because of the secret work that always seems to be going on for the M.O.D. In fact secret scientific work began here as long ago as 1935 with the earliest experiments on radar, before the team of scientists moved down the coast to Bawdsey.

Tides
HW at Orford Quay is 1 hr. after HW Dover.
Range of tide at Springs: 2.4m; at Neaps: 2.0m.

Charts
Admiralty No.2052.
Stanfords No.6 (The Suffolk Rivers).

Facilities
No visitor's moorings.
Water on quay (see Harbourmaster).
Diesel from Chandler near quay.
Petrol from garage in town (1½ miles).

Points of interest
Orford Castle.
Havergate Island Bird-sanctuary.

Sustenance
'Jolly Sailor' (near quay).
'King's Head' (in town).
Butley and Orford Oysterage (restaurant).

3. SHINGLE STREET *(Entrance to the River Ore)*

The entrance to the river Ore seems to fascinate East Coast yachtsmen, even though some of them, like that experienced sailor Hammond Innes, would never venture over the bar. Those that have done so will appreciate the thoughts expressed by Hilaire Belloc in his book 'On Sailing the Sea' after entering the river in an unseaworthy boat that had been built in 1864 and had spent most of her life on the Broads:

'We were racing down the long drear bank of Orford, past what they call 'the life-boat house' on the chart (there is no lifeboat there nor ever was), past the look-out of the coastguard, till we saw white water breaking on the bar of the Alde.' 'Then I said to my companion, 'There are I know two mouths to this harbour, a northern and a southern; which shall we take?' But he said, 'Take the nearest.'

There may still be two ways into the river today and local fishing boats may well use them, but visiting yachtsmen have come to depend upon the annual survey of the entrance by Commander John Pryor. The problem with the entrance is that it is no longer used by commercial shipping and Trinity House, who are economising these days, only maintain one land-mark and one offing buoy. Unfortunately it seldom happens that the configuration of the knolls off Shingle Street allows a safe course to be set on a direct line between the buoy and the beacon.

Before retiring to Snape, Commander Pryor worked for the Hydrographic Department at Taunton and yachtsmen are certainly grateful to him for the sketch charts he makes available each Spring through the Aldeburgh Yacht Club.

Once inside the river, although the tides run hard in the lower reaches, the water is relatively calm, and peaceful anchorages can be found in the Butley River or The Gull on the west side of Havergate Island – where landing is prohibited without permission because it is a well-known bird sanctuary.

Tides
HW at Orford Bar is practically the same as HW Dover.
Range of tide at Springs: 2.5m; at Neaps: 2m.

Charts
Admiralty No.2052.
Stanfords No.6 (The Suffolk Rivers)

Facilities
None nearer than Orford (5 miles from entrance)

Points of interest
Butley River.
Havergate Island Sanctuary (no landing).

Sustenance
None nearby.

4. RIVER DEBEN *(Entrance to River Deben)*

There are signs that the shoals off the entrance to the River Deben are beginning to extend a line that may eventually form the same kind of continuous shingle bank as exists between Orford Ness and Shingle Street. But unlike the single beacon at the entrance to the Ore, there is a pair of leading marks or 'metes' to guide yachtsmen into the Deben. This does not necessarily make things easy, because for the last few years a 'dog-leg' course was necessary to avoid the tip of a shoal extending off the shore to the south of the bar buoy.

Some yachtsmen using out of date charts or pilot books are unaware of the changes and having found the 'metes', simply line them up and proceed to enter. If, as they should be, they are on a rising tide and they touch the bottom, they can usually get off fairly quickly. In any case, help is on hand for those who need it, because the local pilot, Robert Brinkley, keeps a listening-watch on VHF Channel 8, and will come off to see a yacht in if required.

Once inside the shingle knolls, visitors sometimes relax too soon and find themselves aground on the Horse Shoal that sits in the middle of the river between the Felixstowe and Bawdsey shores. It was at Bawdsey Manor that much of the early work on radar was done and a single lattice tower still stands as a memorial to that remarkable achievement.

The sailing club at Felixstowe Ferry mainly concerns itself with dinghy racing and when one of the class meetings is being held, the whole place is alive with young people launching their dinghies from the steep-to shingle beach.

The scene must have looked very different in the middle of the last century, when Edward Fitzgerald ('Old Fitz') was sailing in and out of the river in his schooner, the 'Scandal' with 'Whisper', his dinghy trailing astern. Yet one or two things have remained the same — the Ferry Boat Inn is still there and the ferry will still carry you across to the Bawdsey shore.

Tides
HW at the Deben entrance is 25min. after HW Dover.
Range of tide at Springs: 3.2m; at Neaps: 2.7m.

Charts
Admiralty No.2693.
Stanfords No.6 (The Suffolk Rivers).

Facilities
For moorings, contact boatyard at Felixstowe Ferry.
Fuel: Diesel from yard.
Water, from standpipe in the slipway.
Chandler, adjoining yard.
Club. Felixstowe Ferry SC (mainly dinghies).

Points of interest
The Ferry.
Bawdsey Manor.

Sustenance
The 'Ferryboat'.
The 'Victoria'.
Cafe near boatyard.

5. RAMSHOLT *(River Deben)*

'Mud is beautiful. That's something most people only appreciate when they fall in love with an East Coast Estuary. The most beautiful is the Deben.'
So wrote Hammond Innes in his lovely book 'East Anglia'. Some of the Deben's mud can be seen on both sides of the river at Ramsholt, but landing there at low-water is not too difficult because there is a hard, remaining from the days when a ferry plyed between Ramsholt and Kirton Creek.

At high water, dinghies or even keel boats can lie alongside the stone quay that was once used by smacks and sailing barges. For most yachtsmen, the attraction at Ramsholt is the pub, sadly now without its background of pine trees, lost in the October gale of 1987. Some of us remember the 'Arms' in the days when it was run by Mrs. Nunn, who, if we asked nicely, would let us fill our water cans from the pump in the kitchen. Today, visiting yachtsmen will still be welcomed and because there are no supplies obtainable nearer than Alderton, nearly three miles away, the present

landlord of the Ramsholt Arms will sometimes collect groceries for visitors while they are in the village.

Some writers claim that Ramsholt church has an elliptical, or according to Hammond Innes, an 'egg-shaped' tower. But Norman Scarfe, in the Shell Guide to Suffolk, says: 'The buttressed septaria tower is round, not elliptical: illusion of ellipse created by ancient buttresses that run up to the top'. If you want to make up your own mind, the church is only half a mile from the quay by footpath.

One of the most popular and therefore sometimes congested weekend anchorages on the Deben, is off a small sandy beach known as 'The Rocks'; about a mile up-river from Ramsholt and a mile below Waldringfield.

Tides
HW at Ramsholt Quay is 45min. after HW Dover.
Range of tide at Springs: 2.6m; at Neaps: 2.2m.

Charts
Admiralty No.2693.
Stanfords No.6 (The Suffolk Rivers).

Facilities
Contact Harbourmaster for mooring.
Water from tap at 'Ramsholt Arms'.
No supplies nearer than Alderton.

Points of interest
Church with round (elliptical?) tower.

Sustenance
The 'Ramsholt Arms'.

6. HARWICH HABOUR *(Shotley Point Marina)*

Pepys, who was the Member of Parliament for Harwich for a brief period reckoned that the Harbour was 'the only haven between the Thames and the Humber, and better than either'. For centuries Orwell Haven, as it is sometimes called, was used as a naval base and a mail-packet port, the original service plying between Harwich and the Dutch port of Hellevoetsluis. Today, across the harbour on the Felixstowe shore, passenger ferries sail for Zeebrugge, and container ships from all over the world are constantly on the move, while on the other side of the Stour, Parkestone Quay is the arrival and departure point for the Harwich-Hook and the Scandinavian ferries. But no boats berth now at the old Zeebruge train ferry pier.

Trinity House has had a base at Harwich since 1669, when the first 'buoy-keeper' was appointed. Today all the buoys used to mark the channels and shoals of the Thames Estuary are serviced from Harwich and lightships are moored just inside the River Stour. One of them can be seen in the photograph as well as a Large Automatic Navigational Buoy (LANBY) of the type that it

was thought might replace lightships. However, it proved so difficult to service LANBYs at sea in bad weather, that Trinity House decided, instead, to convert lightships so that they could be serviced on station but be operated without a crew and be monitored and controlled by radio from a station on shore.

On the west side of the River Orwell, just above Shotley Spit and out of the fairway, there is a time-honoured anchorage that is still sometimes used by yachts and the occasional spritsail barge; although not so many craft anchor there since the new Shotley Point Marina was opened in 1989.

On a fine week in summer, hundreds of yachts sail down the Orwell and out of the harbour; some of them bound across the North Sea and others simply out for a day's sail. These amateur sailors must sometimes wonder at the skill and patience of many famous seamen who long ago sailed these same waters without a fore and aft rig to get them to windward or an engine to push them over a foul tide or through a calm patch.

Tides
HW at Harwich is 40min. after HW Dover.
Range of tide at Springs: 3.8m; at Neaps: 3.2m.

Charts
Admiralty No.1491 (Harwich Harbour).
Stanfords No.3 or No.6.

Facilities
No visitors moorings at Harwich.
Temporary berthing in Pound.
Fuel from garages.
Water from town pier.
Shotley Point Marina (All services).
Clubs: Harwich and Dovercourt SC, Harwich Town SC, Shotley SC and Shotley Point YC.

Points of interest
Pilot Station at Pier.
Old Light Towers.
Shipping movements.

Sustenance
The 'Angel' and the 'Three Cups' at Harwich.
'Bristol Arms' at Shotley.
Restaurant on quay and at Marina

7. IPSWICH *(Fox's Marina)*

Ipswich was an important port as long ago as the tenth century and it flourished in Elizabethan times when wool and cloth made up most of its exports. But silting of the upper reaches of the river in the eighteenth century caused a serious decline in trade that was not reversed until the Wet Dock was opened in 1841 — when it was the largest of its kind in Britain. By the middle of the last century, four shipping lines were operating between Ipswich and London, one of them still under sail, while paddle steamers left for Harwich on every tide.

The Wet Dock has never been much used by yachts, although there is now a small marina there. Occasionally the Dock is the venue for a meet organised by the Old Gaffers Association and any of those traditional craft look perfectly at home while moored in front of the Old Custom House.

An Orwell Yacht Club existed in the mid-nineteenth century, but the present Club at Bourne Bridge (seen in the lower left corner of the photograph) was founded in 1918, so there may be a few people around who remember the occasion. If so, they will have seen many changes within sight of the club-house. The most obvious ones being the power station on the opposite shore and Fox's Marina (venue for the annual East Coast Boat Show) on the other side of Ostrich Creek, so named because of the 'Ostrich Inn' nearby.

Further upstream in Cliff Reach a container ship can be seen alongside the West Bank Terminal. Nowadays it is mainly such ships that use the river and since they must stay strictly within the dredged channel to avoid such mud shoals as the Wherstead Ooze just above the Orwell Bridge or the Pond Ooze opposite Freston, yachtsmen have to keep a sharp lookout and not expect steam to give way to sail, as once it did.

Tides
HW at Ipswich is 1hr, 15mins after HW Dover.
Range of tide at Springs: 4.0m; at Neaps: 3.4m.

Charts
Admiralty No.2690.
Stanfords No.6 (The Suffolk Rivers).

Facilities
Some visitor's moorings at Orwell YC.
All facilities at Fox's Marina.
Some berths in Wet Dock.
Stores from shop near Club.
Fuel from nearby garage or marina.

Points of interest
Annual East Coast Boat Show.
Sutton Hoo treasures at Ipswich Museum.

Sustenance
Orwell YC.
Marina YC.
The 'Ostrich Inn'.

8. MISTLEY *(River Stour)*

Mistley has been a port since the 11th century, no doubt because the channel of the tidal Stour runs close under the foot of Furze Hill, where loading and unloading cargo was easier. But Mistley really came into its own when the canal was cut from Brantham to Sudbury in 1713, making it possible to move goods inland without having to use the sometimes impassable roads.

Shortly after that, Richard Rigby built the first of the quays at Mistley and then his son, an eighteenth century entrepreneur, living in high style at Mistley Hall, followed up with warehouses, maltings, a timber-yard and a ship-yard where 'men o' war' of some 700 tons were built. Today, the yard, which can be seen at the eastern end of the quays, is used for breaking rather than building ships.

Rigby also had the idea of turning Mistley into a fashionable resort, commissioning Robert Adam to design a Spa town 'with hot and cold sea-water baths'. The twin towers of a church long since gone can be seen in the bottom left corner of the photograph and these, together with a fountain incorporating a statue of a swan, remain as evidence of Adam's work on the project.

There are plenty of live swans at Mistley and those that can be seen in the photograph are no doubt happily feeding on waste from the maltings.

Mistleymen were famous as 'sailormen', the name given to those who sailed spritsail barges in and out of the rivers and creeks of the Thames Estuary. The most famous of these skippers was Albert (Chubb) Horlock and one of his most memorable races must have been the Thames match of 1903, when Chubb won in the 'Sara', having covered the 54-mile course in 5 hours, 11 minutes and 10 seconds; an average speed of well over 10 knots! Chubb's son Robert tells the stories of his own and his father's time in barges in the marvellous book 'Mistleyman's Log'.

Tides
HW at Mistley is 1hr. after HW Dover.
Range of tide at Springs: 3.4m; at Neaps: 2.7m.

Charts
Admiralty No.2693.
Stanfords No.6 (The Suffolk Rivers).

Facilities
No moorings at Mistley.
Water from quay.
Stores from shops in town.
Fuel from garage.
Train service to Colchester and London.

Points of interest
The Adams Towers.

Sustenance
The 'Anchor' (up the hill).

9. WALTON BACKWATERS *(Titchmarsh Marina)*

Walton Backwaters is the name given to a maze of creeks and islands tucked in behind the relatively high ground of Walton-on-the-Naze.

There has been a yacht club at Walton since 1920, but the real increase in the number of yachts sailing in and out of the Backwaters began with the building of the marina in the Twizzle some fifteen years ago.

Walton Backwaters, the 'Secret Water' made famous by Arthur Ransome's book of that title, is popular because those who wish to go to sea can be there within half an hour, while others, who simply seek some quiet anchorage away from any form of shore-based distraction can find one without having to sail very far.

Before these waters became a haunt of yachtsmen, they were used by sailing barges to reach small quays adjoining farms at such places as Beaumont, Kirby-le-Soken and Landermere, as well as Walton itself, where a windmill once stood on the site of the present Walton and Frinton Yacht Club. All these places dry out soon after high water and the gutways leading up to them snake about so much that a barge could seldom sail right up to a quay without the help of a local 'huffler'.

Not all the quays were used by farmers, the one at the head of Oakley Creek has served an explosives factory on remote Bramble Island since 1906 and, understandably, yachts are not welcome there.

There is an unusually steep-to shingle bank at Stone Point, at the entrance to the Walton Channel and at weekends this spot is always popular because it offers clean landing and the opportunity for a stroll and a picnic.

Tides
HW in the Twizzle is 50min. after HW Dover. Range of tide at Springs: 3.5m; at Neaps: 2.87m.

Charts
Admiralty No.2052.
Stanfords No.4 or No.6.

Facilities
Moorings posts and pontoon outside marina.
Fuel at marina.
Water on pontoons
Chandlery at marina.
Phone (for taxis) at marina.
Customs Office at marina.

Points of interest
Nature Reserve on Skipper's Island.

Sustenance
Hotels and restaurants in Walton-on-the-Naze.
The 'Ship' at Kirby le Soken.

10. BRIGHTLINGSEA *(River Colne)*

Brightlingsea, at the mouth of the River Colne, was a 'Cinque Port Liberty', a sub-port of Sandwich in Kent and at one time this meant that Brightlingsea men were exempted from serving on juries or in the militia.

The men of Brightlingsea have never been afraid of going to sea and abundant evidence of this can be found in the many memorial plaques on the walls of the nave in All Saints church, about a mile from the town. The stark simplicity of some of the inscriptions arouse the emotions of those of us who merely go afloat for pleasure in the summertime. 'John Goddard, lost with his Barge, *Frances,* Flushing to London, December 4, 1896' or 'Leonard Wellum, 17, drowned from his Father's Barge *James Garfield,* off Ramsgate, 1891'.

Some of the larger Brightlingsea smacks used to sail far from their home port, and were away for three or four months at a time, dredging deep-sea oysters off Terschelling, a couple of hundred miles away. Frank Carr, in his classic book 'Vanishing Craft', tells the story of the dismasting of the Brightlingsea 'Skillinger', the *Hawthorne,* in a North Sea gale during February around the turn of the century.

Today, Brightlingsea sailors are mostly cruising and racing types, but the speeds they reach under sail, particularly in catamarans — in which the town specialises – would amaze the old-timers.

Because there is no room for them to swing on a mooring, the larger yachts are moored fore and aft between dolphins, as can be seen in the photograph. Just beyond the moorings in the top left of the picture, a creek winds its way up to St. Osyth and its ancient Priory. There is an old quay at the head of the creek, but boats only remain afloat there for an hour or two around high-water.

The town, seen towards the top edge of the page is Clacton.

Tides
HW at Brightlingsea is 55mins after HW Dover.
Range of tide at Springs: 4.6m; at Neaps: 3.7m.

Charts
Admiralty No.3741 (Approaches to Rivers Colne and Blackwater).
Stanfords No.4 (The Essex Rivers).

Facilities
Mooring between posts (arrange with Harbourmaster).
Fuel from garages in town.
Water from hard or Colne YC jetty.
Chandlers in town.
Sailmaker in town.
Clubs: Colne YC and Brightlingsea SC.

Points of interest
St. Osyth Priory.
Colchester Castle (Bus Service).

Sustenance
The 'Anchor'. Colne YC.
Restaurants in town.

11. WIVENHOE *(River Colne)*

Opposite Wivenhoe the entrance to a creek known as the Roman River can be seen and this reminds us that Colchester is only a few miles away. In those Roman times Wivenhoe must have already been well known for its oysters, since shells of the molluscs have often been found among the kitchen waste of Roman villas. According to Defoe, writing in 1722 — 'The chief place where oysters are now had is Wivenhoe and the shores adjacent — the fishermen who take them at the mouth of what they call Colchester Water and carry them up to Wyvenhoo, where they are laid in beds on the shoar to feed, as they call it; and then, being barrelled up and carried to Colchester, they are sent to London by land'.

Wivenhoe, like so many other places on the East Coast with access to a tidal river, has seen its share of smuggling, but it may have been the only place where contraband was sometimes carried in a fast yacht.

The two Sainty brothers, one the designer and the other the builder, were so highly regarded early in the seventeenth century, that when in 1820, the Marquis of Anglesea wanted a yacht built he had to use his influence to obtain pardons for the brothers, who at the time were both in gaol for smuggling.

The *Pearl*, the 130-ton cutter built for the Marquis was so successful that thereafter Wivenhoe became famous for its yachts. Although the yard was taken over by Thomas Harvey (father of Sir John Harvey, the actor-manager) in 1832, its reputation continued to grow with the building of such famous craft as Sir Thomas Brassey's *Sunbeam* and Edward Fitzgerald's smaller *Scandal*. In his autobiography, Martin Harvey tells of being born into- 'an atmosphere of tar, Oregon pine, the odiferous mud of the River Colne; to the music of the caulker's mallet and the whining steam-saw'.

Rowhedge, seen on the west bank just above the Roman River, had a yard where the Harris Brothers built the Dixon Kemp-designed *Firecrest* in which Frenchman Alain Gerbault sailed around the world single-handed in the 1920s, when such a feat was still considered remarkable.

Tides
HW at Wivenhoe 1hr. 20min. after HW Dover.
Range of tide at Springs: 4.6m; at Neaps: 3.7m.

Charts
Admiralty No.3741.
Stanfords No.4 (The Essex Rivers).

Facilities
All moorings dry out.
Water at quayside.
Fuel from yard or garage in town (½ mile).
Chandlery at yard.
Stores from town.
Train service to Colchester and London.

Points of interest
Colchester Castle.
Nottage Institute (open Sundays in Summer).

Sustenance
The 'Rose and Crown'.
The 'Anchor' at Rowhedge.

12. WEST MERSEA *(River Blackwater)*

West Mersea is such an attractive subject when seen from the air that I feel I need offer no apology for including another shot of it in this edition.

It seems that some Romans, after settling in Colchester only a few miles away, found Mersea Island a pleasant place in which to live and relax, just as many retired people — many of them yachtsmen — have discovered more recently.

As is noted in the piece about Wivenhoe, the Romans liked oysters, although there is no evidence that they cultivated them — simply collecting them from the rivers or creeks as required. It was not until the sixteenth century that Colchester men organised the dredging and cultivation of oysters, and not long after that Mersea followed suit; the scale of their activity steadily growing until by the end of the seventeenth century a Mr. Buxton reported that there were — '130 vessels working within sight of Mersea'.

In her history of Mersea Island, Mary French tells us that in the early 1800s —

'oysters were sold by the tub of two bushels; generally from four shillings to six shillings a tub'. At that time oysters were not a luxury, but by 1942, when Pyefleet oysters fetched the highest price in Europe for three centuries; they certainly were.

It is good to know that the local Sea Scouts are now restoring the old shed on Packing Marsh Island where millions of oysters must have been sorted and packed over the years.

In the foreground of the photograph many handsome yachts can be seen on their moorings, some of them no doubt, helping to uphold West Mersea Yacht Club's tradition as a stronghold of offshore racing on the East Coast.

Tides
HW at West Mersea is 1hr. 10min. after HW Dover.
Range of tide at Springs: 4.3m; at Neaps: 3m.

Charts
Admiralty No.3741.
Stanfords No.4.

Facilities
Moorings arranged with Clark and Carter's or Wyatt's yard.
Diesel fuel from Wyatt's yard
Petrol from village.
Water at top of causeway.
Sailmaker nearby.
Buses to Colchester.
Clubs: West Mersea YC and Dabchicks SC.

Points of interest
Oyster 'shop' on Coast Road.

Sustenance
The 'Victory'.
Restaurant in village (¾ mile).

13. BRADWELL CREEK *(River Blackwater)*

In his book 'Down Tops' 1' Hervey Benham called Bradwell picturesque because — 'the old barge quay, crowned with its towering crooked posts, with the green hill rising behind, is the loveliest of settings for a barge.'

Many of the barges that traded from Bradwell belonged to a local farmer named Clement (Clem) Parker who was renowned for keeping his fleet in perfect condition, rope, paint and varnish were to be had for the asking and once every year each barge spent a week on the 'ways' while all her gear was taken ashore for overhaul. Parker's house flag, or 'bob', incorporated the Oddfellow's insignia — a red heart within a white hand in a blue ground.

The old quay can be seen just above the entrance to the yacht harbour and a few ancient posts remain to remind us of the days when barges were berthed there. Mostly the outgoing freights were grain, loaded into the hold in sacks, or a stack of hay built so high on deck that the mate had to be stationed in the bows to direct his skipper at the helm.

The marina was established in the early 1970s and was soon troubled by silting, but that problem was dealt with by regular dredging and as can be seen from the photograph, there are very few vacant berths now.

The atomic power station has only one thing in its favour in the eyes of most yachtsmen — it does provide a useful landmark from a long way off.

For hundreds of years the 'Green Man' with its white walls, red roof and stone floor, has welcomed anyone fresh in from the sea after negotiating the tricky entrance to Bradwell Creek.

The busyness suggested by this view over the Blackwater should be compared with the peace and quiet conveyed by the photograph I chose for the back cover — taken only a few minutes later.

Tides
HW at Bradwell is 1hr. 10min. after HW Dover.

Charts
Admiralty No.3741.
Stanfords No.4 (The Essex Rivers).

Facilities
Pontoon berths in marina.
Water in marina or from Bradwell Quay YC.
Stores from shop in village.
Fuel from marina.
Buses to Maldon.
Clubs: Bradwell Quay YC and Bradwell Cruising Club (Marina).

Points of interest
Chapel of St. Peters-on-the-Wall (2 miles).

Sustenance
The 'Green Man'.

14. HEYBRIDGE BASIN *(River Blackwater)*

When the Chelmer and Blackwater Navigation Company was formed in 1793, at the height of the period of 'canal fever'; none of its directors could have possibly foreseen that two hundred years later, all of the revenue of the company would come from berthing pleasure boats and none from commercial traffic. The fourteen mile canal was cut between Springfield near Chelmsford and Colliers Reach on the River Blackwater. The original plan had been to start the canal at Maldon, but that Borough opposed the scheme, fearing loss of tolls; so the promoters decided to bypass Maldon and start from Heybridge.

The bridges and locks of the canal were designed by John Rennie, and using a gang of 50 men, the project was completed in three and a half years.

As happened with so many canals, the coming of the railways saw the beginning of a decline in waterborne traffic which continued until most of them fell into disuse. For a short while after World War II some Baltic timber was transferred from ships moored off Osea Island and then taken by canal barge to a wharf at Springfield. At about the same time, an eel merchant stored live eels from Holland in a tank in the Basin before taking them to London by lorry. But all of that has now ended.

The Blackwater is said to be one of the saltiest rivers in Britain and salt making — still carried out at Maldon — once flourished at Heybridge in a works just to the north of the Basin and close to Saltcote Hall.

Now a kind of yacht harbour, Heybridge Basin has long been connected with sailing for pleasure. One of the most famous of all yachts, the 'Jullanar' was owned by E.H. Bentall, a very successful inventor and manufacturer of agricultural equipment, whose original factory building still stands beside the canal at Heybridge. 'Jullanar' was the joint design of Bentall and John Harvey of Wivenhoe and she was remarkable because of a 'cutaway' profile below the waterline, which reduced her wetted surface so that she sailed faster. If Harvey and Bentall could see the fin-keeled yachts of today, they would realise just what they had started.

There is a bonus to be had from using Heybridge Basin as a sailing base, because the bottom of a yacht that is sometimes in fresh and sometimes in salt water collects neither barnacle nor weed.

Tides
HW at Heybridge Basin is 1hr. 30min. after HW Dover.
The range of tide at Springs: 3.7m; at Neaps: 2.4m.

Charts
Admiralty No.3741.
Stanfords No.4 (The Essex Rivers).

Facilities
Moorings in basin or canal.
Water from standpipe near inner lock-gates.
Chandlery from yard near lock.
Club: Blackwater SC.

Points of interest
Maldon (3 miles by canalside walk or by bus).

Sustenance
The 'Jolly Sailor' (quayside).

15. BURNHAM-ON-CROUCH

For many yachtsmen I suppose the most important change at Burnham in recent years was the creation of a marina to the west of the town — seen in the top left corner of the photograph. For many boat-owners, especially families with small children, there is much to be said for lying alongside a pontoon in a marina rather than on a swinging mooring out in the river.

I well remember being marooned on a deep-water mooring at Burnham one wild Easter weekend years ago. Having gone aboard 'Iwunda' on the Good Friday we were unable to safely use the dinghy again until the Monday evening.

For those who still prefer to be moored in the river, there are now five floating pontoons to make life easier and, of course, if you are a member of the Royal Burnham or Royal Corinthian Yacht Clubs, a boatman will put you aboard and take you ashore.

A few years ago there was a long running-dispute, leading to an appeal to the Secretary of State against the Crouch Harbour

Authority's refusal to allow 7000 tonne ships as long as 450 feet, to navigate the river up to the Baltic Wharf at Wallasea on the south bank, opposite Burnham. The appeal was disallowed but in the meantime the river was marked with more buoys than ever before and all of them lit so that ships can reach and leave the Baltic Wharf whatever the time of high water.

Before the proposed Baltic Wharf expansion, the only lit buoy between the Whitaker Beacon and Burnham itself, a distance of some twelve miles, was the Sunken Buxey, but now, yachtsmen entering the river at night have no less than twenty-four light buoys to show them the way.

Although perhaps not as fashionable as Cowes, Burnham Week at the end of August each year provides top class racing for some 400 boats in 20 classes with participants ranging from a 12-Metre ex-Americas Cup contender down to 10.5ft. Cadets.

Tides

HW at Burnham-on-Crouch is 1hr. 20min. after HW Dover.
Range of tide at Springs: 4.9m; at Neaps: 3.4m.

Charts

Admiralty No.3750.
Stanfords No.4.

Facilities

Moorings controlled by four yards plus marina berths.
Landing at four pontoons.
Fuel from pontoon at Essex Marina (opposite Burnham).
Water near most landing places.
Chandler on quayside and in marina.
Sailmaker in marina.
Train service to London.
Clubs: Royal Burnham YC, Royal Corinthian YC, Crouch YC, Burnham SC and United Hospitals SC.

Sustenance

The 'White Hart' Hotel. The 'Anchor' Hotel. Royal Corinthian YC. Restaurants in town.

The Royal Burnham Yacht Club

16. HAVENGORE BRIDGE *(River Roach)*

The 'military' first came to Foulness in the middle of the last century, after a Colonel Shrapnell had persuaded the War Office that the Island should be used as an artillery firing range. Shells have been whizzing over the Malpin Sands ever since, although nowadays such activities come under the Proof and Experimental Establishment of the M.O.D.

Before 1914, when a bridge was built, the only way onto Foulness Island from the mainland was by ferry, pontoon-bridge or, at low water, via the medieval Broomway running parallel to the shore across the sands. Access to the various islands from the Broomway was by steps over the sea wall, the one remaining example being Wakering Stairs.

Throughout the last century spritsail barges loaded bricks for London from brick-fields at Great Wakering, using Havengore Creek as their 'back-door' to and from the Thames. After World War 1, when the first bridge was built, a hand-operated cantilever span allowed the passage of both working craft

and an increasing number of yachts. Despite modernisation by the addition of electric power, the old bridge was considered unserviceable by the mid-1980s and the £5 million bridge seen in the photograph with its lifting span at road level, replaced it in 1988.

Although there is no longer any commercial traffic through Havengore Creek, the short-cut it provides for yachtsmen sailing from Essex and Kent remains very important as it often saves 15 miles or so on a voyage between the River Crouch and the Thames or the Medway.

Once through the bridge and bound for the Roach or Crouch, a yacht has the choice of two routes; to port along Havengore Creek, past the boat-yard at Wakering and through the swing-bridge onto Potton Island or to starboard through Narrow Cuts and the Yokesfleet. The former way is better for Paglesham and the latter for Burnham.

Tides

HW at Havengore Bridge is 1hr. 5min. after HW Dover.
Range of tide at Springs: 4.4m; at Neaps: 3.2m.

Charts

Admiralty No.3750.
Stanfords No.4 (The Essex Rivers).

Facilities

There are no moorings of facilities nearer than Great Wakering or Paglesham.

Points of interest

The 'Broomway' across Maplin Sands.

17. GILLINGHAM and HOO

Although not included in the photograph, half a mile to the east of the swimming pool the evidence remains of several cement works that once bordered the river at Gillingham. Cement was made at many places in this part of Kent, because clay could be obtained from the saltings that abound in the area. The clay, dug and loaded into barges by gangs of 'muddies', was used as a flux when making the cement; a hundred tons of clay (a barge's freight) being mixed with two and half hundred tons of chalk before being burnt.

One by one over the years the cement works on the Medway, reachable only by light-draught boats such as sailing barges, were closed because they could not compete with places like Swanscombe and Northfleet on the Thames, where large bulk carriers can berth.

Two marinas can be seen in the photograph. The one across the river at Hoo might claim to be the first to be established in Britain, as long ago as 1956. The term 'marina' was perhaps a bit grand at that time

because it was applied to a somewhat primitive harbour constructed from a ring of concrete barges within which a miscellaneous collection of craft dried out for most of the time. Facilities then were simple in the extreme, but today, a new yacht harbour with a sill, allows boats to remain afloat all the time and provides them with all the facilities the modern yachtsman expects.

In the foreground can be seen the two sections of the more recent Gillingham Marina, with a couple of mobile cranes still working there. One part of the marina is entered through a lock that can be worked for most of each tide, while the adjoining, original area, is used by those prepared to dry out in soft mud for about half the time.

Tides

HW at Gillingham is 1hr. 40min. after HW Dover.
Range of tide at Springs: 5.4m; at Neaps: 4.4m.

Charts

Admiralty No.1835.
Stanfords No.8.

Facilities

Gillingham: water from eastern arm of pier.
Stores from shops in vicinity.
Diesel from pier.
Petrol from garage near gas-works.
Trains to London.
Hoo: Water from YC.
Stores from shops in village.
Fuel from marina.
Clubs: Medway Cruising Club (Gillingham), Hoo Ness YC and Hundred of Hoo YC.

Points of interest

Riverside walk between Hoo and Upnor.

Sustenance

The 'White House' at Gillingham.
The 'Five Bells' at Hoo.

18. COCKHAM REACH *(River Medway)*

This view from above Upnor, shows a very historic stretch of the river Medway, because on the opposite shore, just out of the picture, are the great basins of Chatham Dockyard. Chatham was originally established as a Naval base by Queen Elizabeth in the sixteenth century — 'for the security of her subjects, and the terror of her enemies.' Elizabeth had feared the Spanish, and when that danger passed, alertness waned so that in June of 1667 the Dutch fleet entered the Thames, captured Sheerness on the 11th, and on the 15th, seven of their ships sailed up as far as Upnor, where they set fire to the *Royal James*, the *Loyal London* and the *Royal Oak*. A chain across the river that should have protected it, was simply unbolted at one end by the Dutch and for years a bolt displayed at Enkuisen in Holland was claimed to be the actual one.

In the eighteenth century, St. Mary's Island, the tip of which can be seen on the right of the photograph, was reclaimed by convict labour to become part of the 80 acres finally occupied by the Dockyard.

When I sailed to Upnor in an old Broads sailing cruiser soon after the Second World War, we left her on an anchor, clear of the few boats moored there and went by bus into Rochester to buy an extra pump. On returning we couldn't see her anywhere, until a longshoreman tapped me on the shoulder, asking 'Have you lost your boat?' On admitting that I had, he replied 'She lifted her anchor, so I put her on an Admiralty buoy over on the Chatham side. It'll cost you salvage.' 'but I've only got five pounds', I spluttered. 'That'll do' came the swift reply.

Times have changed and it would not be wise to drop an anchor in Cockham Reach these days. Today we can see hundreds of craft swinging to moorings on both sides of the river and the Dutchmen that come now, race against the yachts from the Medway Yacht Club, whose beautifully situated headquarters can be seen at this end of the woods.

Tides
HW at Hoo is 1hr. 40min. after HW Dover.
Range of tide at Springs: 5.4m; at Neaps: 4.4m.

Charts
Admiralty No.1835.
Stanfords No.8 (North Kent Coast).

Facilities
Moorings belong to clubs.
Water from Medway YC or Cabin Yacht Stores.
Stores from shop in village.
Fuel from Club.
Chandler nearby.
Clubs: Medway YC and Upnor SC.

Points of interest
View from high ground above Upnor.

Sustenance
The Pier Hotel.
The Waterfront Restaurant.

19. QUEENBOROUGH *(West Swale)*

In Victorian times there was a regular passenger service between Queenborough and the port of Flushing in Holland. Submerged remains of the old piers still form a hazard for any craft venturing too close to the shallows known as the Lappel just to the north of Queenborough itself.

In order to reach Queenborough it was necessary to build a road and rail bridge from the mainland onto the Island of Sheppey at a point about a mile east of Queenborough. Before that time the Island could only be reached by ferry, the last one of which operated at Harty at the eastern end of the Swale.

After World War I, traffic to Holland passed to Harwich, but has recently returned with the twice daily service between Sheerness and Flushing operated by the Olau Line.

Queenborough was founded by Edward III and named in honour of his queen Philippa of Hainult. The town once boasted a castle, but by Elizabethan times it was no more than a small fishing village; Daniel Defoe commented that — 'the chief traders of the Town seem to be Alehouse keepers and Oystercatchers.'

Besides the ferry terminal there is a roll-on roll-off container port at Sheerness and recently the oil terminals over on the Isle of Grain have been converted to accept up to 70,000 containers a year, so that the Medway could soon challenge Felixstowe as the most important terminal on the East Coast.

With this greatly increased commercial traffic it is not surprising that there are no moorings or facilities for yachtsmen at Sheerness — the nearest convenient landing place being on the hard at Queenborough. The moorings at Queenborough are controlled by the Swale Borough Council and they have thoughtfully provided a concrete scrubbing pad with a card-operated power point for a high pressure hose just inside Queenborough Creek. At high water the creek, which runs in behind the town, can be used for taking on water or stores.

Tides
HW at Queenborough is 1hr. 35min. after HW Dover.
Range of tide at Springs: 5.2m; at Neaps: 4.2m.

Charts
Admiralty No.2572.
Stanfords No.8 (North Kent Coast).

Facilities
Moorings controlled by local council.
Two visitors' moorings off hard.
Yard with slip in Queenborough Creek.
Diesel fuel from yard.
Chandler nearby.
Clubs: Queenborough YC.

Sustenance
The 'Flying Dutchmen'.
The 'Old house at Home'.
Queenborough YC.

20. CONYER QUAY *(The Swale)*

My own recollections of Conyer go back to the Great Tide on the last day of January 1963, when *Iwunda*, my 34ft. centre-boarder was wintering at Cooper's yard. She lay outside a barge that was alongside the quay and while the surge landed the barge partly ashore, Iwunda was lucky and undamaged.

That fateful Saturday night must have been alarming for those living nearby who watched the tide rise as high as they had ever seen it before — with another two hours of flood to run! At that time a fellow was living aboard an old gaff cutter called *Our Norah*, and on the Saturday afternoon he had gone down the creek to rescue a marooned wildfowler. Unable to get back except in his dinghy, he had left the cutter on an anchor in South Deep at the entrance to the creek. That night the tide floated *Our Norah* clean over the sea wall and into the marshes near the old Butterfly Wharf. I never did hear how they got her out.

In 'Just off the Swale', Donald Sattin tells the story of village life at Conyer, where some seventy-five sailing barges were built between 1866 and 1914 — the most famous of them being the *Sara*, one of White's 'flyers'. White's yard was on the site that is now occupied by Conyer Marine.

Conyer was not only a barge-building village, but also had extensive brick-works and a cement factory. In fact it is likely that bricks were made there in Roman times. Sattin relates several feats of strength and endurance by Conyer men. A barge arrived at the quay on the tide one day and was loaded with 44,000 bricks before leaving on the afternoon tide next day!

Another story that appealed to me relates to Charlie Cooper who worked at White's yard building barges during the day, but built barge boats on his own account during the evenings; finishing one fourteen foot clinker-built boat single-handed in a week.

Now it is only yachtsmen who frequent the old yards that have been converted into tidal marinas with their floating pontoons. Although so much has changed, the fascination of Conyer and its creek remain.

Tides
HW at Conyer Quay is 1hr. 30min. after HW Dover.
Range of tide at Springs: 4.6m; at Neaps: 4.0m.

Charts
Admiralty Nos.2571 and 2572.
Stanfords No.8 (North Kent Coast).

Facilities
Water from boatyards.
Stores from chandler.
Diesel oil from yards.
Sailmaker nearby.
Clubs: Conyer Crusing Club.

Points of interest
Kentish countryside (hop-fields and orchards).

Sustenance
The 'Ship Inn'.

21. OARE CREEK *(Hollow Shore)*

Yachts and boats of all kinds line the east bank of Oare Creek, berthed alongside stagings or pontoons; all of which dry out for much of the time. The creek, rather more than half a mile long, runs from the village of Oare to its junction with Faversham Creek at Hollow Shore, a favourite haunt of 'traditional' yachtsmen, who tend to sail smacks or bawleys. Many of these traditionalists belong to the Old Gaffers Association or the Kentish Sail Association, organisers of the annual Swale Smack and Barge Matches.

'The Shipwright's Arms' at Hollow Shore operates without mains electricity, water or drainage, but offers a unique vantage point from which to observe the movements of any craft bound in or out of the two creeks — and to voice friendly criticism from the comfort of the public bar.

Although it dries out above Hollow Shore, Faversham Creek is still used by small coasters, which keep alive the centuries old traditions of the ancient port of Faversham, where cargos as diverse as wine, wool and gunpowder were once handled.

Three or four hundred years ago, Faversham was an important centre for the manufacture of gunpowder, supplies of which were used at Trafalgar and Waterloo. The 16th century Chart Gunpowder Mill is still preserved and can be found off Stonebridge Way.

Today the quays at Faversham are mostly occupied by yachts, many of them undergoing overhaul or conversion with much of their gear temporarily put ashore on Iron Wharf, just below the great 'Oyster Bay' warehouse that reminds us of the earlier trading days.

The entrance to Faversham Creek, leading to Oare Creek, is just inside the east Swale, close to Harty Ferry. A spit that extends from the western side of the entrance is marked by a north-cardinal buoy, while the rest of the winding gutway is also marked by unlit buoys.

The village of Oare at the head of that creek is just over a mile from Faversham Station but is connected by a bus service so that it can be reached fairly easily by rail and road from London.

Tides
HW at Hollow Shore is 1hr. 25min. after HW Dover.
Range of tide at Springs: 4.6m; at Neaps: 4.0m.

Charts
Admiralty No.2571.
Stanfords No.8 (North Kent Coast).

Facilities
Water from boatyard.
Stores from chandler.
Fuel: Diesel from yards.
Bus from Oare to Faversham (1 miles).
Clubs: Hollow Shore Cruising Club, Kentish Sail Association (Hollow Shore).

Points of interest
Nature Reserve (Hagden Marshes).
Chart Gunpowder Mills (Faversham).

Sustenance
The 'Shipwright's Arms' (Hollow Shore).
Three pubs in Oare.